DATE DUE

A to Z

Egypt

BY JEFF REYNOLDS

children's press®

A Division of Scholastic Inc.
New York Toronto London Auckland Sydney
Mexico City New Delhi Hong Kong
Danbury, Connecticut

Consultant: Dr. Amy J. Johnson, Ph.D., Berry College
Series Design: Marie O'Neill
Photo Research: Candlepants Incorporated
Language Consultant: Beatrice Gruendler, Yale University

For Paul Sergio
– J.R.

Egyptian lemonade recipe provided by touregypt.net

The photos on the cover show the Great Pyramids at Giza (left), King Tutankhamen's gold death mask (right), a Nile crocodile (bottom), and an Egyptian girl (center).

Photographs © 2004: Art Resource, NY/Werner Forman Archive: 13 top; Corbis Images: 15 left, 28 bottom, 37 right (AFP), 13 bottom (Archivo Iconografico, S.A.), 9 bottom (Dave Bartruff), 32 inset (Bettmann), 4 top, 35 top right (Gianni Dagli Orti), 32 top, 33 left (Hulton-Deutsch Collection), 4 bottom (Joe McDonald), 17 bottom left, 24, 34 (Richard T. Nowitz), 30 (Carmen Redondo), 28 top (Jeffrey L. Rotman), 8 bottom (Royalty-Free), 6 top, 11 left (Sean Sexton Collection), 12 bottom, 25 bottom (Peter Turnley), 33 right (Sandro Vannini), 5 top left (Kennan Ward), 5 bottom (Roger Wood); Corbis SABA/Thomas Hartwell: 16 bottom; Corbis Sygma/Amet Jean Pierre: 14; Envision Stock Photography Inc./Steve Needham: 11 right; Getty Images/Jean-Claude Aunos: 15 right; ImageState: 31 (Peter Pinnock), 5 top right (Adrian Pope); Index Stock Imagery: 23 (AbleStock), 29 (Steve Starr); Kenneth Garrett Photography Inc.: 9 top left; Magnum Photos: 27 (Abbas), 10 top, 16 top (Ian Berry); National Geographic Image Collection/Stephen St. John: 6 bottom; Photo Researchers, NY: 17 bottom right (Barbara Strnadova), cover bottom (Karl H. Switak), 8 top (Laura Zito); PictureQuest: cover top left, 22 (Philip Coblentz/Brand X Pictures), 7 (Hisham F. Ibrahim/Photodisc), 17 top (Steve Starr/Index Stock Imagery); Stone/Getty Images/Will & Deni McIntyre: 18, 19; Superstock, Inc./Neal & Molly Jansen: 10 bottom; The Image Bank/Getty Images: 25 top left (Frans Lemmens), cover center (Guido Alberto Rossi); The Image Works: cover top right (Michael Justice), 37 left (Tatsuo Kume/HAGA), 25 top right, 36 (Josef Polleross), 9 top right, 38 (Science Museum, London/Topham-HIP), 35 center (The British Museum/Topham/HIP), 12 top (Topham Picturepoint), 26 (Charles Walker/Topfoto).

Library of Congress Cataloging-in-Publication Data

Reynolds, Jeff.
  Egypt / by Jeff Reynolds.
    p. cm. — (A to Z)
  Includes bibliographical references and index.
  ISBN 0-516-23652-0 (lib. bdg.)   0-516-25070-1 (pbk.)
  1. Egypt—Juvenile literature. I. Title. II. Series.
  DT49.R493 2004
  962—dc22

                          2004003279

1 2 3 4 5 6 7 8 9 10 R 13 12 11 10 09 08 07 06 05 04

Contents

The god Anubis had the head of a jackal (left). The god Horus had the head of a falcon (right). Do you see a jackal and falcon on these pages?

This is a black-backed jackal.

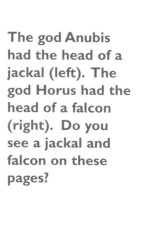

Animals

Jackals, falcons, camels, cats, and other animals live in Egypt today. But, animals were important in Ancient Egypt, too.

Falcons are meat-eating birds.

Some Egyptians still ride camels for transportation.

Gods are shown with human bodies and animal faces. Anubis was a god who helped souls find their way in the **afterlife**. He is usually shown with the head of a jackal. Jackals are dog-like animals that live in many parts of Africa. The sky-god **Horus** had the head of a falcon. Falcons are related to hawks and eagles.

Cats lived in ancient Egypt, too. They first became people's pets during the time of the **pharaohs**. People even made statues of cats.

5

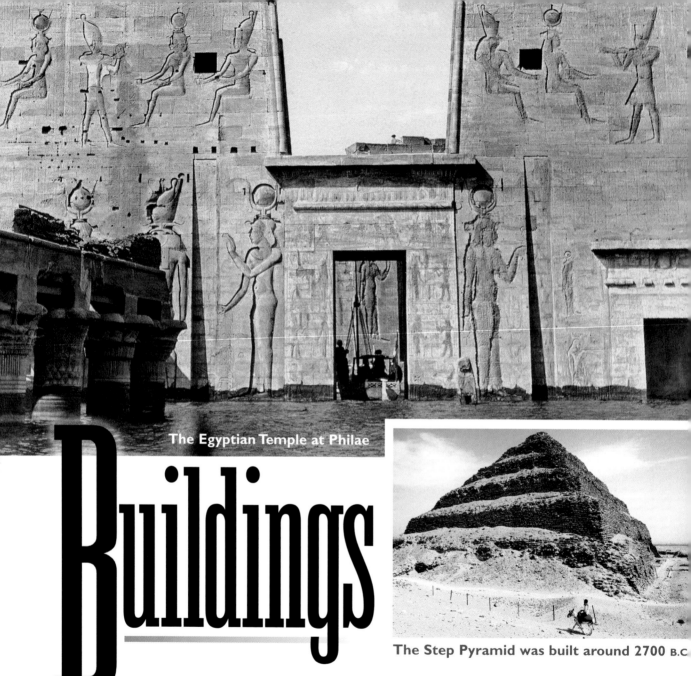

The Egyptian Temple at Philae

Buildings

The Step Pyramid was built around 2700 B.C.

Egypt has the oldest stone building in the world. It is the Step Pyramid, a **tomb** that was built nearly 48 **centuries** ago. It is unusual because the sides form "steps." They do not look smooth like most of the other pyramids in Egypt. **Archaeologists** believe it was built in this shape to help the buried pharaoh climb back to the sky. The walls inside many tombs and temples are filled with drawings. They show people doing brave deeds and living everyday life. The drawings also tell stories about gods visiting the earth.

The Nile River flows through central Cairo.

Cities

kubrii

(kuh-brye)
means bridge in Arabic.

Cairo is Egypt's capital city. It is the largest city on the African continent. There are huge skyscrapers and highways in Cairo. The Nile River connects Cairo with the Mediterranean Sea. Alexandria is Egypt's second-largest city.

Dress

Today, many Egyptians dress in much the same way as North Americans do. However, some still wear traditional clothing.

Bedouin women in traditional desert clothing. Their eyes are also outlined with kohl.

These boys are wearing modern clothing.

Queen Nefertari shown with kohl-lined eyes

This is what a kohl pot looked like in ancient times.

Turbans can be made from linen, cotton, or silk.

Men who work in the hot desert sun wear long, loose robes with hoods called **galabiya**. Women wear long gowns called **abeyya**. Some people wear turbans on their head. Some Egyptian women cover their head and arms with a scarf to observe their religion.

As a part of their dress, men and women in Ancient Egypt outlined their eyes with **kohl**. Kohl is black coloring.

9

Egyptian workers on a gas platform in the Mediterranean Sea

Egyptian farmers began growing cotton during the 1800s.

Exports

Fuels such as oil and natural gas are Egypt's most important exports. Egyptian cotton is prized around the world for its high quality. Some types of fruit, such as **dates**, are also exported. By law, part of the food grown by Egypt's farmers must stay within the country. Egypt's population is growing and needs this food.

Egyptian Lemonade Recipe

WHAT YOU NEED:

- 6 cups water
- 2 unpeeled lemons, quartered
- 5 tablespoons sugar
- 1 tablespoon orange blossom water (*mazahar*)

HOW TO MAKE IT:

Add the lemons to the water and bring to a boil. Cover and simmer for 20 minutes. Strain into a teakettle and stir in the sugar and mazahar. Bring to a boil and serve. You can add honey instead of sugar for variety.

Look how Egyptians sold lemonade long ago.

Food

Lemonade is still a popular drink in Egypt. Street vendors roam city streets selling it. Ask an adult to help you with this recipe for lemonade.

Gamal Abdel Nasser

Government

President Hosni Mubarak

Gamal Abdel Nasser was an important leader in Egypt. He is remembered for helping to make Egypt a republic. He was Egypt's president from 1956 until 1970.

Today, Hosni Mubarak is the president of Egypt. He has been elected president four times. President Mubarak works closely with other world leaders to solve conflicts peacefully.

In Egypt, laws are written by the People's Assembly. This is a group of 454 people who are elected by their communities or are appointed by the president.

12

A piece of the
head of a statue
of Hatsheput.

History

We also know about Egypt's history
from pictures like this one. This shows
how people farmed.

People who study the past divide the history of Ancient Egypt into kingdoms. The kingdoms are divided into periods of time when different groups of people ruled Egypt. For most of Egypt's history, the ruler was called the pharaoh.

**Youssef Chahine
makes movies.**

Important People

People who work in the arts share
the culture of Egypt with the rest of
the world.

Actress Faten Hamama is showing one of her awards.

Naguib Mahfouz is another great artist. He writes prizewinning novels about Egyptians.

Youssef Chahine is Egypt's best-known filmmaker. He was born in Alexandria, but he later moved to California. He writes, directs, and sometimes acts in his films.

Actors and actresses such as Faten Hamama have helped make Egyptian films loved around the world. Her movies deal with issues that women face in Egypt today.

Egypt's farmers depend on water from the Nile River to grow food.

People use computers to do their work at the Cairo Stock Exchange.

Jobs

About one-third of Egypt's people are farmers. Water from the Nile River has helped farmers grow more food. Some Egyptians provide services to people in banking and tourism. Some people work in manufacturing jobs. They produce **textiles**, such as cloth made from Egyptian cotton.

Keepsakes

Open-air markets can be found nearly everywhere in Egypt. They are small, outdoor stores like the farmers' markets found in many American cities. Street vendors sell food, clothing, and keepsakes.

Tourists may look for a vendor who sells **scarabs**. In ancient times, some scarabs were used to stamp symbols onto documents. They are named after the scarab beetle.

This is what a real scarab beetle looks like.

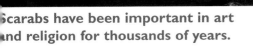

Scarabs have been important in art and religion for thousands of years.

17

Land

The **Sahara** Desert covers nearly two-thirds of Egypt. The Egyptians call it the Western Desert. The Arabian Desert is in the east.

The Nile River is more than 4,000 miles (6,400 km) long. It is the longest river in the world.

The Nile River flows between the two deserts. It flows toward the Mediterranean Sea. People have been growing food for thousands of years along the banks of the Nile. As the Nile empties its water into the Mediterranean, it spreads **fertile** soil onto an area of land. This land is known as the Nile River Delta. This area is one of the richest farming **regions** in the world. Most of the people in Egypt live on a thin strip of land on either side of the Nile River.

nahran-Niil

(al nahr an-Nile) means The Nile in Arabic.

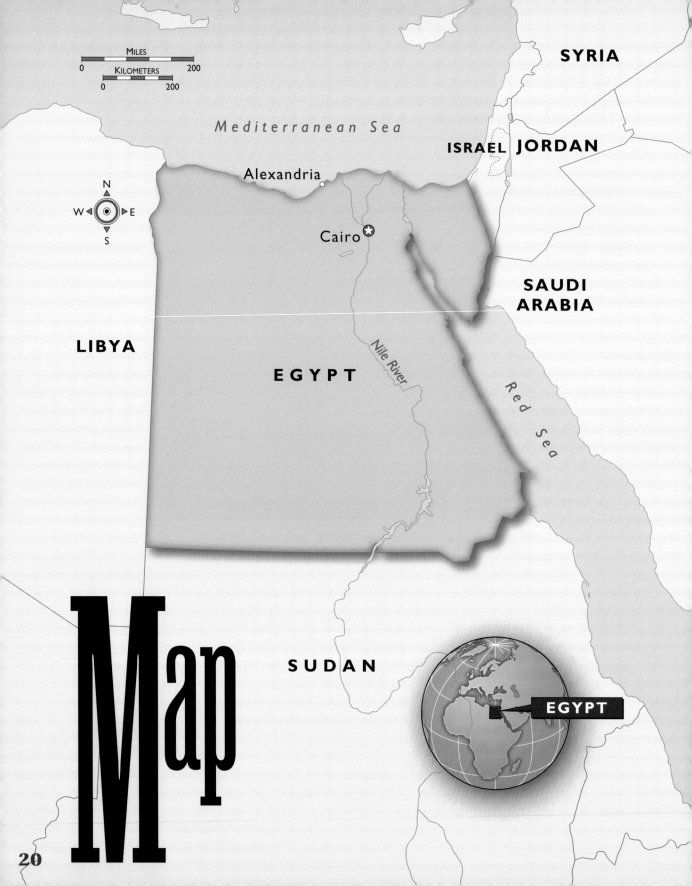

SYRIA

Mediterranean Sea

ISRAEL JORDAN

Alexandria

Cairo ★

SAUDI
ARABIA

LIBYA

EGYPT

Nile River

Red Sea

SUDAN

Map

EGYPT

Nation

In ancient times, Egypt was much larger than it is today. Now, Egypt is slightly larger than the states of Texas and New Mexico together. The nation's official name is the Arab Republic of Egypt.

The flag of Egypt is red, white, and black. The black stripe at the bottom stands for the Egypt of long ago. Modern Egypt is represented by the white stripe in the center. The red stripe at the top stands for the people of Egypt. Egypt's national symbol is in the center of the flag.

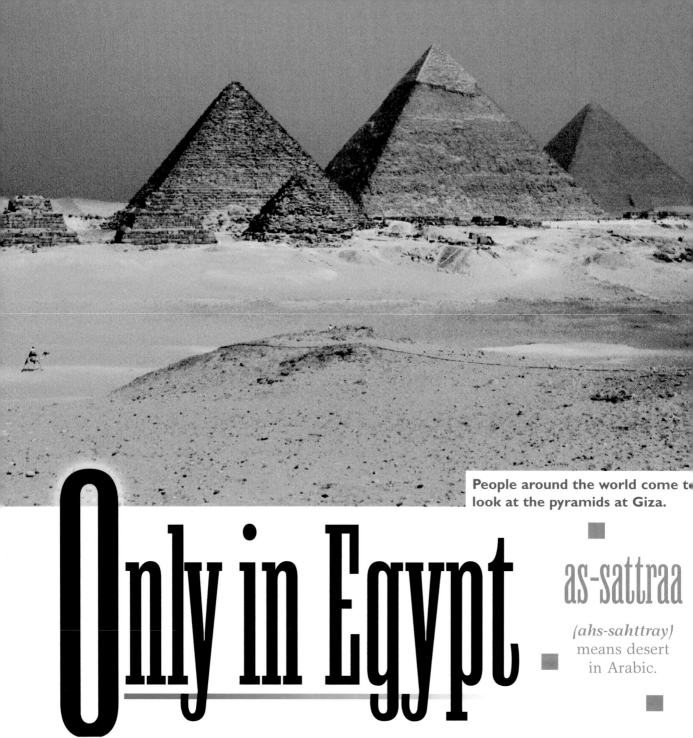

People around the world come to look at the pyramids at Giza.

Only in Egypt

as-sattraa

(ahs-sahttray) means desert in Arabic.

Pyramids can also be found in other parts of the world. However, Egypt is the only country in the world where you can see the Great Sphinx.

The Arabic name for the Great Sphinx is *abu al-khof*. It means "Father of Terror."

The Great Sphinx is an enormous statue. It has the head of a man and the body of a lion. It is taller than ten people standing on each other's shoulders. Most people believe that the face of the Great Sphinx was modeled after the pharaoh Khafre. The statue guards the way to his pyramid.

Egypt has many smaller statues that look like the Great Sphinx. Some of them have bodies of other animals or the face of a woman. None of them is as famous as the Great Sphinx.

This fellahin father and his children are a rural Egyptian family.

People

Most people who live in Egypt are Arabs. Egypt's many peasants, or poor farmers, are known as *fellahin*.

Egyptians live in different kinds of homes. This is a small house in the town of Amba Bishol.

More than half of the country's people live in small villages and farming communities. Most of these villages are near the Nile River. The peasant people who live and work there are known as *fellahin*. The fellahin who live and work there have begun to move to the larger cities in search of work. Often, there is no space for them because the cities have become very crowded.

A section of an illustrated papyrus scroll

Question What Is Papyrus?

Papyrus is a plant that was once found in great quantities along the banks of the Nile River. It grew to be nearly 13 feet (4 m) tall. Its strong stem was shaped like a triangle. For thousands of years, papyrus was used by people to make everything from boats to clothing. Its most important use was for making of paper. Much of what we know about the ancient Egyptians we have learned by reading their papyrus **scrolls**. Today, the papyrus plant has almost disappeared from Egypt.

Many Muslims go to a mosque for Friday prayers.

Religion

Most of the people who live in Egypt are Muslims. Muslims are followers of the religion of Islam. Muslims believe in one God. They also believe in praying five times each day. If possible, these prayers are said in a **mosque**. A mosque is a Muslim place of worship. Daily prayers may be said anywhere, as long as the person praying faces in the direction of **Mecca**. Mecca is a holy city to Muslims. Some laws in Egypt are based on Islamic law.

School & Sports

Children in Egypt begin school when they are about six years old. They must stay in school until they reach the age of 15. After that, about half of them drop out of school. Those who stay in school can look forward to a free education all the way through college.

Soccer is the most popular sport in Egypt. Students begin playing it at a very early age. Egypt is home to several professional soccer teams.

A donkey cart joins busy city traffic.

Transportation

In busy cities like Cairo and Alexandria, there are donkey carts in traffic jams along with taxis and trucks. Few people in Egypt own cars. They get around on buses, subways, bicycles, or by walking. All types of boats, ships, and ferries help make the Nile River a busy highway. EgyptAir is the national airline. Its planes fly from Egypt to many countries around the world.

These large statues of Ramses II were once almost entirely buried under the desert sand.

Unusual Places

Egypt is filled with sights that can only be seen by going under the ground. The Valley of the Kings is one of those places. Visitors can tour many underground tombs of the pharaohs.

Once, you nearly had to go underwater to see one of Egypt's most unusual sights. When the **Aswan High Dam** was built in southern Egypt, some historic **sites** were in danger of becoming flooded. The temple of Abu Simbel was moved to higher ground. Its enormous statues of Ramses II were cut into pieces and put back together away from the water.

as-samak

(ahs-sahmahk)
means fish
in Arabic.

Visiting the Country

Coral reefs in the Red Sea

The Red Sea lies to Egypt's east. It is more than 1 mile (1.6 km) deep in some places. Along its shallow edges are beautiful **coral reefs**. Divers can view brightly-colored coral and schools of fish. Tourists can also see the reef by taking a ride in a glass-bottom boat. There is also a special submarine made for sightseeing.

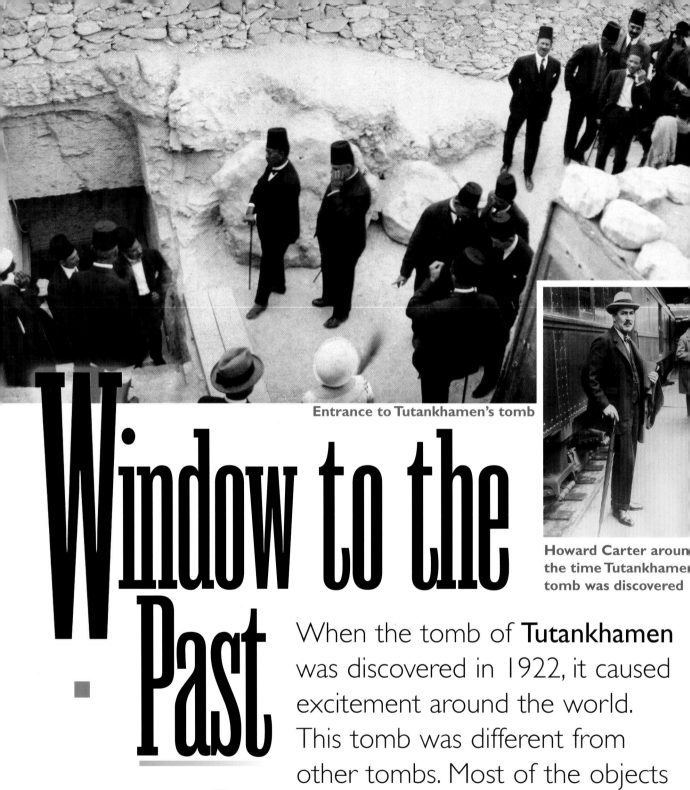

Entrance to Tutankhamen's tomb

Howard Carter around the time Tutankhamen's tomb was discovered

Window to the Past

When the tomb of **Tutankhamen** was discovered in 1922, it caused excitement around the world. This tomb was different from other tombs. Most of the objects buried with the young king were still inside.

Carter opening the tomb of Tutankhamen

This gold coffin holds the internal organs of Tutankhamen.

Long ago, thieves would break into tombs and steal the valuable items that had been buried with the mummies. Tutankhamen was buried in a tomb that was very small for a pharaoh. Thieves never thought to look for treasure in it. A man named Howard Carter decided to look anyway. Carter was a British scientist. Some of the things he found in the tomb were a golden throne, beds and couches, weapons, board games, and the bodies of the pharaoh's two baby daughters.

The mummy of Ramses II, a pharaoh who died 3,000 years ago

X-tra Special Things

The liver, intestines, lungs, and stomach of mummies were put in these special jars (below). They are called canopic jars. The jars were buried with the body.

Mummies of important people, such as rulers, were placed in decorated rooms.

Mummies have been found around the world, but Egypt's mummies are special. We know a great deal about how and why they were created.

Ancient Egyptians believed that a person who died would need his or her body in the afterlife. So, bodies needed to be **preserved**. One way to preserve something is to dry out all of its moisture and keep it dry. The dry climate of Egypt has helped to preserve mummies very well. We have a good idea how some famous Egyptians looked when they were alive by studying their mummies.

Stick dancing is a popular sight during moulids.

Yearly Festivals

Moulids are festivals that celebrate the birthdays of saints and holy people. During a moulid, people enjoy feasts, parades, and other entertainment.

A woman prepares food for an iftar.

Picnics are held to celebrate Sham al-Nessim.

iHtafala
(ihtah-fah-la)
means to
celebrate in Arabic.

Sham al-Nessim, which means "Scent of the Breezes," is a popular springtime celebration. Both Muslims and Christians enjoy having picnics on this day.

Ramadan is the most important month of the year for Egypt's Muslims. During Ramadan, adults stop eating during the day. This is known as fasting. Muslims do this out of respect for a special time in their history and to show their faith in God. After sundown, the fasting stops, and people enjoy a meal called **iftar** with families and friends.

An Egyptian water clock

Zamaan

Zamaan is an Egyptian word that means time. Some ancient Egyptians used a water clock to tell time. Water would drip slowly out of a small hole in the bottom of a stone container. Lines on the inside of the container showed how much time had passed since the container was filled.

Think about time when you think about Egypt. Think about the amazing things from long ago that are here for us to see today.

■ Arabic and English Words

abeyya The long gown worn by Egyptian women

abu al-khof The Arabic term for the Great Sphinx, meaning "Father of Terror"

afterlife The place to which a soul goes after a person has died

archaeologists (ar-kee-OL-uh-jists) Scientists who learn about the past by finding and studying objects from long ago

Aswan High Dam A large dam built on the Nile River near the southern Egyptian city of Aswan

century (SEN-chuh-ree) A period of 100 years

coral reefs Rocky formations made up of the skeletons of small sea animals called corals. Coral reefs provide shelter for living coral and fish

date (DAYT) The sticky, brown fruit of the palm

fellahin (fel-uh-HEEN) Peasants; farmers

fertile Good for growing healthy plants

galabiya (ga-lay-bye-yuh) The long hooded robe worn by Egyptian men

Horus (HOR-uhs) The hawk-headed Egyptian god of the sky

iftar The meal served at the end-of-day during Ramadan

kohl (kuhl) Black coloring used to highlight the shape of one's eyes

Mecca A city in Saudi Arabia that is considered holy by Muslims because it is the birthplace of Muhammad. Muhammad was a prophet and the founder of Islam

mosque (MOSK) A Muslim place of worship

moulids Holidays that celebrate the birth of holy people

papyrus (puh-PYE-ruhss) A plant from which paper was made in ancient times

pharaoh (FARE-oh) The supreme ruler in ancient Egypt, believed at times to be a god

preserve To make something last for a long time

Ramadan (RAHM-i-dahn) A month-long holiday that celebrates God's gift of the Qur'an, the holy book of the religion of Islam

region (REE-juhn) An area or district

Sahara A large desert covering much of northern Africa, including about two-thirds of Egypt

scarabs Symbolic objects shaped like scarab beetles

scrolls Rolled-up pieces of paper or hide on which something has been written

Sham al-Nessim A popular springtime celebration in Egypt.

sites Places of interest, especially to people who study history

textiles Cloth products that are manufactured from natural or human-made material.

tomb A building that covers and protects a grave

Tutankhamen Pharaoh of Egypt 1370-1352 B.C.

zamaan An Egyptian word meaning time

■ Let's Explore More

Egypt by Tom Streissguth, Carolrhoda Books, 1999.

Egypt, A True Book™ by Elaine Landau, Children's Press, 2000.

Look What Came From Egypt by Miles Harvey, Franklin Watts, 1998.

Websites

http://www.ancientegypt.co.uk/menu.html
Improve your vocabulary and learn more about famous structures in this website sponsored by the British Museum.

http://touregypt.net/kids/History.htm
Fun games, activities, and stories about Egypt may be found at this web site, sponsored by the magazine Tour Egypt Monthly.

Index

Italic page numbers indicate illustrations.

Meet the Author

JEFF REYNOLDS was raised on a farm in Illinois. He has lived in Minneapolis-St. Paul, New York City, and Connecticut, and now lives and works in Washington, D.C. He received a B.A. from Western Illinois University and an M.A. in Theater History and Criticism from Brooklyn College. At various times he has been a farmer, milk man, school custodian, housepainter, hotel bellman, stamp dealer, teacher, librarian, actor, journalist, and editor. He is also the author of A to Z books about Germany, Japan, Puerto Rico, and the United States.